Alligator

my favorite animal

Published in the United States of America by Cherry Lake Publishing
Ann Arbor, Michigan
www.cherrylakepublishing.com

Reading Adviser: Marla Conn MS, Ed., Literacy specialist, Read-Ability, Inc.
Book Design: Jennifer Wahl
Illustrator: Jeff Bane

Photo Credits: © Personal Story Photo / Shutterstock.com, 5; © marktucan / Shutterstock.com, 7; © Orhan Cam / Shutterstock.com, 9; © Jne Valokuvaus / Shutterstock.com, 11; © Dale Stagg / Shutterstock.com, 13; © Catcher of Light, Inc. / Shutterstock.com, 15; © Svetlana Foote / Shutterstock.com, 17; © Tony Craddock / Shutterstock.com, 19; © Jay Yuan / Shutterstock.com, 21; © Heiko Kiera / Shutterstock.com, 23; © Ozerina Anna 2-3, 24; Cover, 1, 6, 16, 20 Jeff Bane

Library of Congress Cataloging-in-Publication Data

Names: Loh-Hagan, Virginia, author.
Title: Alligator / by Virginia Loh-Hagan.
Description: Ann Arbor : Cherry Lake Publishing, [2017] | Series: My favorite animal | Audience: K to grade 3. | Includes index.
Identifiers: LCCN 2017000943| ISBN 9781634728362 (hardcover) | ISBN 9781634729253 (pdf) | ISBN 9781534100145 (pbk.) | ISBN 9781534101036 (hosted ebook)
Subjects: LCSH: Alligators--Juvenile literature.
Classification: LCC QL666.C925 L64 2017 | DDC 597.98/4--dc23
LC record available at https://lccn.loc.gov/2017000943

Printed in the United States of America
Corporate Graphics

table of contents

About the author: Dr. Virginia Loh-Hagan is an author, university professor, former classroom teacher, and curriculum designer. She's scared of alligators. She lives in San Diego with her very tall husband and very naughty dogs. To learn more about her, visit www.virginialoh.com.

About the illustrator: Jeff Bane and his two business partners own a studio along the American River in Folsom, California, home of the 1849 Gold Rush. When Jeff's not sketching or illustrating for clients, he's either swimming or kayaking in the river to relax.

looks

Alligators are big **reptiles**. They can be 15 feet (5 meters) long. They can weigh 1,000 pounds (454 kilograms).

They have **scutes**. Scutes are bony plates. They're like **armor**. Their skin is hard.

They have a strong tail. It is long. They have strong jaws. They have a **snout**. Their snout is wide. It is rounded.

There are two types of alligators. One lives in the United States. They're larger. The other type lives in China. They're smaller.

Alligators live in rivers. They live in ponds. They live in **swamps**. They like muddy water.

Alligators eat once a week. They will eat anything. They eat fish. They eat snakes. They eat small **mammals**.

Alligators hunt. They wait for **prey**. Then, they catch it. They bite down. They drag prey to the water. They drown it. Then, they eat.

Alligators live in groups. They **bask** in the sun. They walk on land. They can be fast. But they get tired quickly.

They swim well. They use their tails. They can stay underwater a long time.

Females make nests on land. They lay 35 to 50 eggs. Soon the eggs hatch. Moms put babies in their mouths. They carry them to the water.

glossary

armor (AHR-mur) covering that keeps a person or animal safe

bask (BASK) to lay out in the sun

mammals (MAM-uhlz) animals that have hair and give birth to live babies; their body temperature stays the same no matter where they live

prey (PRAY) animals that are hunted for food

reptiles (REP-tilez) animals that have scales and creep on the ground or close to it; their body temperature changes with the air around them

scutes (SKYOOTS) bony plates

snout (SNOUT) nose and mouth of an animal that stick out

swamps (SWAHMPS) areas of soft, wet ground

index